Living with

AUTISM

DR SUNG MIN, LENA HENG,
MAGDALENE FOO, KHENG JOO LIAN

mc Marshall Cavendish
Editions

Illustrations: Julie Davey
Series designer: Bernard Go

First published 2003 by Times Editions

This 2015 edition published by
Marshall Cavendish Editions
An imprint of Marshall Cavendish International
1 New Industrial Road, Singapore 536196

Other Marshall Cavendish Offices
Marshall Cavendish Corporation. 99 White Plains Road, Tarrytown NY 10591-9001, USA • Marshall Cavendish International (Thailand) Co Ltd. 253 Asoke, 12th Flr, Sukhumvit 21 Road, Klongtoey Nua, Wattana, Bangkok 10110, Thailand • Marshall Cavendish (Malaysia) Sdn Bhd, Times Subang, Lot 46, Subang Hi-Tech Industrial Park, Batu Tiga, 40000 Shah Alam, Selangor Darul Ehsan, Malaysia

Marshall Cavendish is a trademark of Times Publishing Limited.

National Library Board, Singapore Cataloguing-in-Publication Data
Sung, Min, 1968- author.
Living with autism / Dr Sung Min, Lena Heng, Magdalene Foo, Kheng Joo Lian; illustrations, Julie Davey. – Second edition. – Singapore: Marshall Cavendish Editions, 2015.
pages cm – (Living with)
"First published 2003 by Times Editions."
ISBN: 978-981-4634-17-5 (paperback)

1. Autism. 2. Autistic children. I. Title. II. Heng, Lena, 1978- author. III. Foo, Magdalene, author. IV. Kheng, Joo Lian, author. V. Davey, Julie, illustrator. VI. Series: Living with.

RJ506.A9
618.9285882 — dc23   OCN 913312294

Printed in Singapore by Markono Print Media Pte Ltd

Dedicated to
all the children of the Child Guidance Clinic
and their parents

CONTENTS

PREFACE

Autism is something very close to my heart and I have been working with this population for more than 10 years. Persons with Autism Spectrum Disorder (ASD) have to cope with a wide range of difficulties. While many make notable improvements with support over time, they face different challenges at various stages of life.

Support services in Singapore have grown significantly over the last 10 to 15 years. Developmental paediatricians from the KK Women and Children's Hospital and National University Hospital are skilled in early diagnosis and assessment of these children. The Adult Neuro-Developmental Service at the Institute of Mental Health supports adults with ASD. We have early intervention centres, special schools and adult centres catering to this population. The Ministry of Education has developed a team of Allied Educators to support these children in mainstream schools. Voluntary welfare organisations like the Autism Association of Singapore and the Autism Resource Centre champion their needs. Public awareness is improving with increasing media coverage and activities like the annual World Autism Awareness week organised by students from the Duke-NUS Graduate Medical School. Tertiary institutions, such as the National University of Singapore and the National Institute of Education, actively engage in local research in autism.

When the Child Guidance Clinic first started developing specialised services for ASD in 2006, we saw about 70 new cases annually. The Neuro-Behavioural Clinic (Autism Services) currently has over 300 referrals to our clinic a year. We have also refined our focus over time to specialised diagnostic assessments and managing children and adolescents with ASD and co-morbid mental health issues. We do active parent education and run training for fellow professionals in ASD. We have also incorporated ongoing research projects with our clinical services to provide a vibrant centre with different options available for our patients.

This book has been authored by a multidisciplinary team of professionals from our clinic (past and present), each with their own skill set to offer. It incorporates updated knowledge on ASD and the clinical experience our team has gained from our last 9 years of specialised practice. We also seek to offer information on the local scene and services available in Singapore to provide practical support for parents here. While knowledge in ASD and developing services for this population is certainly still a work in progress, we look forward to a better future for all persons with ASD and their families.

Dr Sung Min
July 2015

INTRODUCTION

Autism Spectrum Disorder (ASD) is a lifelong neuro-developmental disorder, typically diagnosed between the ages of 4 and 5. Recent prevalence studies point to an increasing trend worldwide. A study on global prevalence for autism in 2010 reported a rate of 7.6 per 1,000 or one in 136 individuals diagnosed with ASD. There are no prevalence studies on ASD done in Singapore to date. However, there is an estimated prevalence of 24,000 individuals with ASD in our population of 4 million, with 5,472 children under the age of 19 years. Approximately 216 new cases of children with ASD are diagnosed annually.

Persons with ASD face social-communication difficulties and have accompanying rigid and stereotypical behaviours. These result in a huge impact on their lives and that of their caregivers. A Ministry of Health study in 2009 using WHO's Disability Adjusted Life Years (DALYs) showed that child and adolescent mental health disorders contributed to three of the top five conditions in youths under the age of 15, with ASD having the highest disease burden, impacting patients and caregivers significantly in all aspects of life, such as financial burden, quality of life, and mortality rate.

In line with the Ministry of Social and Family Development's Enabling Masterplan (2012-2016), we hence must work towards developing the autonomy and independence of persons with ASD, empowering their families in their journey, taking on an inclusive approach and integrating them into society. This book hopes to contribute to this vision by giving an overview of ASD and providing strategies and resources for families and professionals to support them on their journey with their children.

CONCEPTS OF AUTISM
SPECTRUM DISORDER (ASD)

PART 1

Autism is a fairly new concept which has only been recognised for the last 70 years. Our understanding of Autism Spectrum Disorder (ASD) has evolved over the years and will continue to do so as ongoing research broadens our knowledge base of this intriguing developmental disorder. While current descriptions of autism focus on behavioural presentations, research on the biological basis of autism is now taking the forefront.

1.1 THE HISTORY OF ASD

In 1943, Leo Kanner, a paediatrician and psychiatrist in the United States, described eleven children who struck him as sharing "fascinating peculiarities". The children exhibited:
- echolalia (repeating what was previously said),
- an anxious desire to preserve sameness,
- repetitive behaviours,
- a general lack of awareness of other people's existence,
- a lack of ability to play imaginatively with other children,
- pronoun reversal,
- failure to use speech to communicate.

Some of these children functioned at an impaired level in many aspects, even though they gave an impression of normal intelligence. Kanner adopted the term "early infantile autism" to describe these children. At about the same time, a Viennese paediatrician Hans Asperger described children who were quite similar to Kanner's patients and labelled their difficulties as "autistic psychopathy".

In the 1950s and 1960s, Swiss psychiatrist Bruno Bettelheim theorised that children became autistic because of their cold "refrigerator mothers". This has since been shown to be untrue. There was also controversy over the nature of the disorder as it was confused with schizophrenia in adults, which was also described by Bleuler, another Swiss psychologist, as autism. This led to clinicians using terms like '"childhood schizophrenia" and "infantile psychosis" to describe autism.

Recent studies suggest that there is a neuro-biological basis for ASD. This has led to the general acceptance of ASD to be a spectrum of disorders originating in the brain, rather than just a set of behaviours or due to the individual's environment.

1.2 CLASSIFICATION OF ASD

There are two sets of criteria that are currently used worldwide:
- The ICD Classification of Mental and Behavioural Disorders.
- The Diagnostic and Statistical Manual of Mental Disorders (DSM).

In the early 1970s and 1980s, these two classifications had different concepts of autism, although the diagnostic criteria for the disorder were similar:
- The ICD considered autism as "psychosis with origin specific to childhood".
- The DSM viewed autism as part of a group of disorders called the Pervasive Developmental Disorders.

These two sets of diagnostic criteria have changed over the years as people's understanding of autism grew.

Today, the ICD-10 has a classification for "Childhood Autism" while the DSM-5 combines the previous DSM-4 classifications of Pervasive Developmental Disorder Not Otherwise Specified, Asperger's Syndrome and Autistic Disorder into a single category of Autism Spectrum Disorder (ASD). This collapsing of three distinct categories into one group in the DSM-5 classification has been based on research findings suggesting that there is no clear delineation between the categories but rather a spectrum of disorders with varying presentations.

In this book, we will use the term Autism Spectrum Disorder (ASD) to refer to this spectrum of developmental disorders.

PRESENTATION OF ASD

PART 2

Autism Spectrum Disorder (ASD) is a range of disorders of development. There is impairment in social interaction, verbal and non-verbal communication and repetitive or restrictive behaviours. A diagnosis of ASD can be made when symptoms are observed to be present in the early developmental period, although in some cases, symptoms may not be obvious till social demands exceed the individual's capacity to cope. These difficulties cause clinically significant impairment in the individual's functioning. These impairments should also not be better explained by other disorders, disabilities, or developmental delays.

ASD has often been diagnosed much more frequently in males than in females, with a ratio of 4:1. Research has suggested that this may be likely because females with ASD present differently from males and might be often overlooked in diagnosis.

Children with ASD do not display a fixed set of symptoms. This means that one child's symptoms may be different from another and the symptoms may also vary in their severity. The symptoms may also combine in a unique way for each child, thereby producing different sets of problems or difficulties among children with ASD. For this reason, this is considered a "spectrum" of disorders.

2.1 SIGNS AND SYMPTOMS OF ASD

Children with ASD suffer impairments in the areas of:

- social communication and interaction,
- restricted and repetitive activities and interests.

In addition, some children also display difficulties in motor activities, intellectual functioning, as well as general developmental delay. However, only the first two criteria are specific and diagnostic for ASD.

Social Communication and Interaction

Many children with ASD do not develop functional speech. Verbal children with ASD may often display some idiosyncrasies such as echolalia ("parroting" words), repetitive speech patterns, pronominal reversal and the use of neologisms (made-up words). Many have difficulty having reciprocal conversation. Children with ASD are also often very literal in their speech and they may have difficulties in understanding sarcasm, witty puns or metaphors. They may lack spontaneity in sharing interests and experiences with others.

Children with ASD also have difficulties in understanding social cues. Many lack the intrinsic skills that help them engage in social interaction. One characteristic is that these children have difficulty establishing appropriate eye contact or using communicative gestures in their interaction with others. At times, they seem to be unaware of other people's emotions and may unintentionally say or do things that are socially inappropriate. They may also have difficulties in perspective-taking, finding it difficult to understand that another person may not be feeling or thinking the same way or about the same thing as themselves. Many have difficulties initiating interactions with others or establishing and sustaining friendships with their peers.

Restrictive and Repetitive Activities and Interests

Children with ASD may have strong, restricted interests, such as in animals, maps or vehicles. They may have very strong preferences for doing only a few repetitive specific activities like spinning objects or arranging things in a particular order. They may also display motor mannerisms, such as flapping their hands or spinning movements. Some children may have a need to adhere to specific routines without being flexible and may become quite upset if there is a change in their routine. They may either seek or avoid specific sensory stimuli, such as certain sounds, smells, touch or sight. In addition, they may not engage in imaginary activities and pretend-play in the same way their peers might do.

Some signs and symptoms that a child with ASD may exhibit include:

- difficulty in expressing needs,
- engages in odd ritualistic movements such as rocking,
- laughs, cries or shows distress for reasons not apparent to others,
- temper tantrums,
- prefers to be alone,
- difficulty in mixing with other children or adults,
- unable to relate to others in socially appropriate ways,
- not responsive to normal teaching methods,
- not responsive to verbal cues/acts as if deaf although hearing tests are in the normal range,
- sustained play and special interest with certain toys or objects,
- over-sensitive or under-sensitive to pain,
- noticeable physical over-activity or extreme under-activity,
- uneven gross/fine motor skill development.

While these symptoms may suggest a need for further assessment, they may not be specific to ASD. Furthermore, because ASD is based on a range, rather than a clear-cut presence or absence of symptoms, the difficulties and impairments mentioned might also not be present in all individuals with ASD. There might also be a difference in severity and some individuals might have great difficulties in some areas while seemingly being unaffected in other areas.

2.2 PERVASIVE DEVELOPMENTAL DISORDERS
In the DSM-4 diagnostic criteria, Pervasive Developmental Disorder was an umbrella of disorders covering Autistic Disorder, Asperger's Syndrome, Rett's Disorder, Childhood Disintegrative Disorder, and Pervasive Developmental Disorder Not Otherwise Specified

Asperger's Syndrome
This describes a group of children with social interaction difficulties and a pattern of repetitive, rigid interests and behaviours. There is normal cognitive and language development.

Rett's Syndrome
This is a rare disorder that occurs mainly in girls. The child develops normally in the first six to 18 months, but after that shows a change or regression in skills and abilities. There is also a characteristic repetition of gestures or movements like hand-wringing that seem apparently meaningless.

Childhood Disintegrative Disorder
This is an extremely rare disorder. There is a very clear regression in many areas of functioning such as loss of bowel control or language skills after two years or more of normal development which is not due to any other injury or trauma.

Pervasive Developmental Disorder Not Otherwise Specified (PDDNOS) / Atypical Autism
This covers the group of individuals who do not fully meet the criteria of the symptoms that are used to diagnose Autistic Disorder, Asperger's Syndrome, Rett's Syndrome and Childhood Disintegrative Disorder.

As mentioned earlier, the new DSM-5 has brought together these formally distinct disorders into a single category of Autism Spectrum Disorder (ASD). Individuals who may have difficulties in social communication and interaction, but fail to meet the criteria for an ASD diagnosis, may be diagnosed to have Social Communication Disorder.

2.3   THEORIES OF AUTISM

The Mindblindedness Theory
In psychology, the "theory of mind" refers to the ability to infer other people's thoughts, beliefs, desires or intentions. This ability is an important requirement for understanding the behaviour of others. If we understand someone else's beliefs and desires, we can use that understanding to predict how that person will feel.

The mindblindedness theory postulates that the individual with ASD has difficulty with the "theory of mind" and is, hence, unable to put himself into other people's shoes and make predictions about how others will behave. This leads to poor social cognitive skills, which explains why the person with ASD often appears to "act strangely" or behave inappropriately in social settings.

The Executive Dysfunction Theory
In this theory, the individual with ASD is believed to have difficulties with the cognitive tasks that are required for normal social interaction. This means that the individual may have problems with attention shifting, planning, working memory, impulse control, inhibition and mental flexibility, as well as for the initiation and monitoring of actions. This may sometimes explain difficulties in ASD children such as organising their activities or relating events in a clear sequence.

The Theory of Weak Central Coherence
In this theory, it is assumed that the individual with ASD finds it more challenging to put together individual parts to form a whole and "cannot see the wood for the trees". Hence, the individual may have trouble making sense of the complexities of normal social behaviours and, as a result, have difficulties in social situations. For instance, the ASD child may be more interested in a speck of dirt on his teacher's spectacles than the lesson that the teacher is delivering.

The Neural Connectivity Theory

Imaging of the brain has found differences in the activation, signalling and connectivity between the brains of individuals with autism and that of the general population, meaning that individuals with ASD are likely to process information differently from the general population.

All these theories may actually be related to each other in the sense that they explain the deficits that individuals with ASD have at different levels. For instance, because of executive dysfunction, the person has difficulty with putting individual parts to form a whole and because of this, he appears to lack a "theory of mind". These are all also related to the fact that the brain of the individual with autism functions differently from that of the general population and hence leads to the individual's differences in processing of information and in reaction to stimuli.

CASE STUDY

Wei Ming was a Primary 2 student in a Singapore mainstream school. His parents were concerned that he had difficulty coping with language in school and did not have any friends.

Wei Ming started walking at 14 months of age and was using single words at 2 years old. He developed an early interest in reading and was picking out and reading road signs by the time he was 4 years old. However, he was unable to comprehend books that were age-appropriate even though he could read the words. He was very interested in buses and knew in detail the models and routes each bus service took. He had a large collection of toy buses at home and enjoyed spending hours lining them up according to their year of manufacture.

He often spent recess alone in the school library, looking at picture books of vehicles. Being clumsy, he was often left out of games. He would not tell his parents about his experiences and school events.

At the clinic, Wei Ming was diagnosed to have ASD. Psychological assessment showed that he had poor verbal abilities, although he had good non-verbal skills. His parents and teachers were given information on the difficulties in ASD and intervention strategies, such as the use of structure, schedules, work systems and social stories. Wei Ming was also linked to his school's Allied Educator for additional support in his school and he was assigned a buddy in class. His teachers and classmates began understand and support him better in school over time.

ASSESSMENT AND DIAGNOSIS FOR ASD

PART 3

3.1 "RED FLAGS" FOR ASD

All babies and toddlers in Singapore undergo routine developmental surveillance with their general practitioners (GPs) and paediatricians or at polyclinics. As such, delays or deviances in development should be picked up and appropriate referrals initiated. Parents should alert their healthcare professional should they note any of these "red flags" in developmental milestones:

- No babbling, pointing or other gestures by 12 months of age.
- No meaningful words by 18 months of age.
- No spontaneous (non-echoed) two-word phrases by 24 months of age.
- Any loss of language or social skills at any age.

3.4 THE DIAGNOSTIC PROCESS

Concerns about a child's development and possible Autism Spectrum Disorder (ASD) can first be addressed at the Primary healthcare level with a general practitioner, polyclinic doctor or paediatrician. All schools are also linked to community mental health REACH (Response Early intervention and Assessment in Community mental Health) teams. Primary healthcare physicians and REACH professionals will be able to assess the need for referral for further evaluation.

Assessment for ASD should be done by professionals who have a good understanding of ASD. Examples of such professionals include paediatricians, psychiatrists and psychologists. Diagnosis of ASD is based on clinical judgment and there is currently no biological test, such as blood tests or brain scans, for ASD. The diagnostic process may include:

- Parent interview (birth and development, social behaviour, communication skills, patterns of behaviour, learning and education, family history etc).
- Child assessment (direct observation, cognitive/developmental/speech and language assessments).
- Medical examination (physical examination, hearing tests, genetic testing if indicated, others).
- Observation in relevant environments if indicated (such as at home, in school or childcare).

There are certain tools that professionals may use to help them assess children for ASD in a standardised, structured manner. However, these diagnostic tools are not essential for diagnosis and should be seen as useful adjuncts in the whole process. Diagnosis of ASD is made based on the professional's clinical experience, observations and understanding.

There are two main types of diagnostic tools — those that require parents to answer questions about their child and those that are based on observing the child.

Examples of diagnostic parental interviews include:
- the Autism Diagnostic Interview – Revised (ADI-R),
- the Diagnostic Interview for Social and Communication Disorders (DISCO).

Examples of diagnostic observation instruments include:
- the Autism Diagnostic Observation Schedule 2 (ADOS-2),
- the Childhood Autism Rating Scale (CARS).

3.5 GETTING A DIAGNOSIS

Getting a child diagnosed with ASD is not just "labelling" the child. Getting an early diagnosis will lead to early intervention. It is now widely accepted that early intervention improves the outcome for children with ASD. Having a diagnosis of ASD also allows:
- the family, school and other parties supporting the child to understand his behaviours,
- appropriate intervention and educational placement,
- the use of ASD specific strategies to support the child and manage behaviours,
- access to support from various resources, such as ASD-specific programmes, Allied Educators in Singapore schools and voluntary welfare organisations.

UNDERSTANDING
THE CAUSES OF ASD

Diagnosis of Autism Spectrum Disorder (ASD) to date has been based on behavioural presentations and not on biological markers. This reflects the limited understanding clinicians currently have on the causes of ASD. As such, much research is being done to understand the causes of ASD. Improvements in technology over the years offer the hope that researchers will gradually achieve a better understanding of the disorder, leading to more comprehensive and effective diagnosis and management for ASD.

4.1 GENETICS

Studies suggest that there is a genetic influence in ASD. Some genes have been linked to ASD but the nature of this link is still not clear. Recent studies indicate that there are multiple genes involved. There is a high recurrence rate in siblings of 2–10%. Twin studies suggest a concordance rate of 60% to 90% in identical twins. Relatives may also have higher rates of learning, language, social or other mental health problems. We can interpret this to mean that there is a clear genetic influence for ASD.

4.2 BRAIN ABNORMALITIES

New brain imaging technology, such as functional magnetic resonance imaging (fMRI) and positron-emission tomography (PET) has allowed researchers to study the brain in greater detail. However, there is still much to understand about the brain in a person with ASD. To date, studies suggest that:

- about one-third of children have abnormal brain waves,
- there are imbalances in certain brain chemicals, such as serotonin and dopamine,
- certain areas of the brain, such as the limbic system, are correlated with autism,
- some persons with ASD have a larger brain volume,
- persons with ASD have difficulty performing social or emotional tasks on functional brain imaging,
- there are differences in the activation, signalling and connectivity between the brains of individuals with ASD and that of the general population.

4.3   BIRTH EVENTS

Some factors associated with the occurrence of ASD:

- Mother's age.
- Father's advanced age.
- Premature birth.
- Bleeding during pregnancy.

4.4   VACCINATIONS

The Rubella immunisation, which is one component of the Measles-Mumps-Rubella (MMR) vaccination, was once postulated to be linked to the development of ASD. There were also concerns with regards to Thimerosal, a mercury-containing preservative used in vaccinations. This was due to a study done in 1998 at the Royal Free Hospital in London that suggested a link with the MMR vaccination.

However, subsequently researchers have found that withdrawal of the MMR vaccination and Thimerosal has not resulted in reduced rates of ASD. As such, there is no evidence of causality to ASD and parents should bear in mind that the benefits of vaccinations far outweigh any risks.

CONDITIONS ASSOCIATED WITH ASD

PART **5**

5.1   CONGENITAL AND MEDICAL CONDITIONS ASSOCIATED WITH ASD

Autism Spectrum Disorder (ASD) is a neuro-developmental disorder. Some congenital (birth-related) conditions have been associated with ASD, including:

- Tuberous Sclerosis.
- Fragile X Syndrome.
- Neurofibromatosis.
- Phenylketonuria.
- Congenital Rubella.
- Down's Syndrome.

There is also a higher incidence of epilepsy (fits) in persons with ASD. Studies have suggested that about 30% of persons with autism would have epilepsy in their lifetime, with the peak incidence during the first year of life and in adolescence. Epilepsy is a medical condition that needs professional attention. Medication can be prescribed to manage this condition.

5.2   LEARNING AND ASD

Many people with ASD can have intellectual disability. Studies have shown that about 75% of people diagnosed with Autistic Disorder have intellectual disability. They are also more likely to have stronger non-verbal than verbal abilities.

However, there are people with ASD who have learning abilities in the average range and above and may be considered to be "high-functioning". Some people consider those with Asperger's Syndrome to have high-functioning autism. The DSM-4 regarded Asperger's Syndrome as a separate category from Autistic Disorder. However, researchers have found no meaningful difference between Asperger's Syndrome and Autistic Disorder. Hence in the current DSM-5 classification, all sub-categories have been placed under ASD. Children in this category have good language abilities and intelligence but have difficulties in social interaction and lack intuitive knowledge of how to approach others.

Generally speaking, children with ASD respond and learn well with visual presentation of information. They may comprehend information better if the information is presented in the form of pictures, symbols and/or writing. They also do better with clear structure in their environments and daily schedules.

5.3   MENTAL HEALTH IN ASD

People with ASD have difficulties in social communication and have a repetitive, rigid pattern of behaviours. These characteristics will predispose them to stressors in their daily lives as they cope with social demands and adjust to changes in their environment.

Studies now suggest that up to 70% of persons with ASD will experience at least one mental health disorder in their lifetime. Examples include Attention Deficit Hyperactivity Disorder (ADHD), Obsessive-Compulsive Disorder, anxiety, tics, and depression.

Attention Deficit Hyperactivity Disorder (ADHD)

ADHD encompasses two main types of symptoms, namely inattention and hyperactivity/impulsivity. Inattentive symptoms include difficulties sustaining attention, being easily distracted, making careless mistakes, not listening and following through instructions, losing things, being disorganised and forgetful. Hyperactive/impulsive symptoms manifest as being fidgety, being constantly on the move, walking about in the classroom, having difficulty waiting and being talkative.

ADHD may be sometimes difficult to ascertain in children with ASD as issues such as learning difficulties and social abilities may also need to be considered. However, 25–50% of children with autism can have ADHD. Identifying ADHD in children with ASD is important as behavioural strategies and medication can help.

Anxiety

Many children with ASD have difficulty expressing themselves verbally or are unable to explain their needs and feelings clearly. They find social interactions difficult and unpredictable. They may also get worried when their routines are disrupted or when faced with new situations. All these problems may make them anxious. Symptoms of anxiety include being worried, feeling tired and tense, irritability, having difficulty concentrating and sleeping. Up to 80% of persons with ASD may experience anxiety at some point of their lives.

Identifying the stressors and modifying environmental triggers would help to allay anxiety. Teaching some coping strategies, relaxation techniques and medications can also be helpful.

Obsessive-Compulsive Disorder

Obsessions and compulsions are thoughts and rituals that are repetitive and intrusive. They cause distress to those involved and there is relief from anxiety once the compulsions are "completed".

Many children with ASD have repetitive behaviours that are similar to obsessions and compulsions. Examples would include the need to follow certain routines such as arranging objects in a particular order. Most of these obsessions and compulsions are part of ASD and it may not be possible to completely eliminate them. However, these behaviours may need to be managed if they interfere with the child's ability to learn and participate in daily activities. Some of these behaviours can be managed with behavioural strategies. Occasionally, medication may also be considered.

Tics

Tics are sudden, repetitive, involuntary movements or vocalisations. Examples of motor tics are eye-blinking, head jerks or shoulder shrugs. Vocal tics could range from humming and throat-clearing sounds to more complex sounds like vocalising vulgarities.

Because tics can be exacerbated by emotions such as stress or excitement, it will help to modify the environment appropriately so as to minimise the triggers. Medication may be considered if tics are severe and result in significant disability.

Depression

Mood disorders have been reported to occur in up to 30% of people who have ASD. Depression is more likely to be found in adolescents with better cognitive abilities. This is often when the individual gains insight into his social-communication difficulties.

Symptoms of depression include a low mood, lethargy, insomnia, changes in sleep, weight and appetite, poor concentration, inability to enjoy activities and sometimes, suicidal thoughts. Support from family and friends is important. Behavioural and psychological intervention strategies may be helpful. In some cases, medication can help alleviate the depression.

CASE STUDY

Razak was a 15-year-old teenager diagnosed with Asperger's Syndrome while he was attending Secondary 3 in a mainstream school. He had a strong interest in politics and enjoyed discussions on current affairs with his peers, although they found him boring. He did well academically and corrected his classmates and even teachers when they made mistakes. He spoke with proper grammar and a formal British accent.

As such, Razak's peers seldom included him in activities after school. During class projects, Razak had difficulty fitting into a group. While Razak strongly desired friends, he could not understand why he could not have any close relationships with his classmates. He sensed that he could not "fit in with the crowd". He lost motivation in school and this affected his concentration and academic results. He became irritable, tense and slept poorly. He felt a loss of meaning to life.

Razak was diagnosed to have depression by his psychiatrist. He was prescribed medication and was referred for cognitive behavior therapy with a psychologist. He also learnt relaxation techniques, social skills and perspective taking. Razak's teachers were informed of his difficulties and of appropriate strategies to support him in the classroom setting. Razak showed good progress over a year and his medication was tailed off.

MANAGING
PROBLEM BEHAVIOURS

PART 6

Managing and coping with problem behaviours in children with Autism Spectrum Disorder (ASD) involves more than just an understanding of the basic principles of what's often called "behaviour modification or management". There is no quick-fix programme or therapy centre that can solve problem behaviours without the commitment of parents and caregivers. It is not so much of what the therapist does during the intervention sessions but how much parents and caregivers are willing to alter their perception of the "problem" and then, to put in the energy and effort to reinforce the skills taught at home.

Broadly speaking, behaviour management alone may not be able to address all types of problem behaviours. There are certain harmful behaviours where the priority might be to protect the safety of the child or people around him, for which relying on behaviour management alone, may not be effective.

This chapter aims to help parents link knowledge to action for behaviours that are not harmful in themselves but, nonetheless, are considered problematic, difficult or inappropriate in so far as they affect the daily functioning of the child and/or his family.

6.1   SHIFT IN THINKING

"Please stop doing that!"
"Why can't you behave normally?"

Parents and caregivers may often exclaim these phrases in exasperation when they are unable to correct certain behaviours in their child. Perhaps then, those exclamations and unintended hurtful remarks are a signal to stop and think about what is the message that the problem behaviour is trying to convey, or what kind of need does the behaviour seem to serve for the child.

Functional behavioural assessment is based on the premise that all behaviour serves some purpose. The observed behaviour is often the tip of the iceberg and a direct result of underlying issues and/or deficits. Deficits or impairments in ASD include rigid and inflexible thinking, lack of empathy and understanding of the perspectives and intentions of others, poor social interaction and communication skills.

Four Common Functions of Problem Behaviours:
- Attention-seeking
- Wanting something or an activity.
- Avoiding/escaping an activity, person or place.
- Automatic reinforcement (Restricted Repetitive Behaviours).

A. Attention-Seeking

Attention-seeking behaviours often involve wanting an adult's or peer's attention. They may involve some physical action (kicking, throwing things, spitting, hurting somebody etc) or vocal attention (shouting, crying, laughing, swearing etc). The common response from others would then be to pay attention to the child. The ASD child often does not know the socially appropriate way to get attention nor is he able to distinguish the difference between getting good attention or bad attention from others. For instance, pulling down one's pants in front of others will often cause shocked reactions and loud exclamations, or even giggles from peers and sibling—that in itself, is pretty much attention sought and attained.

B. Wanting Something or an Activity

Engaging in a problem behaviour is often a "quick and dirty" way for a child to get what he/she wants—which is a preferred object (e.g. toy) or a preferred activity (e.g. play). Sometimes, parents give in because they cannot tolerate the intensity and frequency of the behaviour.

C. Avoiding/Escaping an Activity, Person or Place

Avoidance or escape-type of behaviours can be exhibited when the child wants to get away from doing an activity (e.g. homework), from a person or people (e.g. don't want social interaction), or from a place (e.g. crowded, noisy environment).

D. Automatic Reinforcement of Restricted Repetitive Behaviours

Automatic reinforcement of behaviours refers to stereotypic behaviours that are common in children with ASD. Research in this area seems to suggest that the repetitive behaviours may provide some form of self-stimulation, self-calming or sensory stimulation. They are often called "stims" and are truly the hardest to eliminate completely, given the physiological nature of the function. Minimising the problem may be the best solution in such cases. Common "stims" include flapping arms, excessive vocal sounds, making tapping sounds with fingers etc. Some ASD children may also engage in repetitive activities such as watching a video clip over and over again, or going up and down an escalator repeatedly.

Parents will notice that when they attempt to stop their child from engaging in one particular repetitive behaviour, the "success" is often short-lived. More often than not, the child gets frustrated and begins to exhibit other forms of undesirable behaviours, or he may discover other forms of repetitive behaviours to replace the previous one.

CASE STUDY

John is a ASD teenager. His mother banned him from watching the "Silly Orange" Youtube clip repeatedly. This resulted in frequent anger outbursts and arguments between John and his mother, which was more draining emotionally and psychologically for both parties.

John's mother brought him to the clinic for intervention. The psychologist mediated a compromise where clear boundaries and limits were set each week for watching the video clip. John's mother came to accept that her ASD child will always exhibit some odd but harmless stereotyped behaviors and learnt to love him just the same. Over time, the relationship between John and his mother improved because she no longer perceived the behaviour as a problem.

If you can identify the possible purpose(s) of the behaviour, you will find yourself shifting in terms of your thinking of the problem behaviour. You will be in a better position to implement strategies or even make changes to reduce the occurrence of the behaviour. A psychologist or therapist who has professional expertise in behavioural interventions, could also help parents to systematically identify possible functions that the problem behaviours serve.

Reflecting on the following questions can also help you to examine the factors that might be reinforcing the behaviours:

- Why is your child resorting to such behaviours to get what he wants or needs?
- Is the difficult behaviour currently the easiest way for him to get what he wants or needs?
- Can you make some changes to serve his wants or needs so that he does not have to resort to doing annoying things?
- Is your child's motivation to engage in the behaviour very strong simply because there is some level of deprivation?
- Is it worth the time and energy to get rid of the behaviour?
- What is the quality of life for your child?

6.2   ANALYSING THE PROBLEM BEHAVIOUR

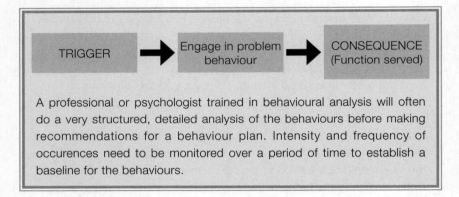

A professional or psychologist trained in behavioural analysis will often do a very structured, detailed analysis of the behaviours before making recommendations for a behaviour plan. Intensity and frequency of occurences need to be monitored over a period of time to establish a baseline for the behaviours.

It is best to enlist the help of a professional to work out a behaviour plan for more complex behavioural problems. A simplified version sequence of events is illustrated by the following case study:

CASE STUDY

Eddy was bored (trigger) in class and often pulled down his pants (problem behaviour) to elicit attention from the teacher and classmates (attention-seeking function served).

How Behaviour Management Works:

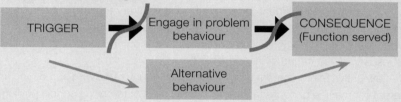

Eddy's psychologist analysed his behavior and highlighted that his teacher needed to have the chain or pattern of events to be disrupted while allowing Eddy to attain his function of seeking attention from peers and adults. Eddy's teacher was advised to give him a class duty or responsibility that created positive attention for him. She then rewarded him with intense praise and encouragement in the presence of his classmates. In the behaviour plan, an alternative behaviour was taught, so that Eddy got positive attention instead of negative attention.

Eddy soon learnt to enjoy the positive attention he got from helping out in class and this reduced the frequency of him pulling down his pants in class.

6.3 CONSISTENT PLAN/PROGRAMME

Having a consistent plan or programme means having identified the function or purpose of the problem behaviour and being prepared to set up a plan that you will be committed and tenacious enough to follow through. "It will often get worse before it gets better" — this adage is based on what behavioural scientists call an "extinction burst".

Pick your battles. Target one problem behaviour to work on for a start. Encouragement, positive reinforcement and rewards are cornerstones of behavioural therapy. They are used intensively when teaching new behaviours.

On the other hand, it may also be necessary to have some negative reinforcement for the undesirable behaviours. This does not mean punishing the child but rather, it provides some logical consequences for the child so that he learns to associate the undesirable behaviour with undesirable consequences.

There are positive and negative types of reinforcement.

Positive reinforcement in essence, means strengthening a behaviour by **adding** something to the environment, e.g. giving praise and tangible rewards. When we need to extinguish a particular behaviour quickly, it is sometimes necessary to use negative reinforcement.

Negative reinforcement weakens a behaviour by **removing** something from the environment, e.g. confiscating a favourite object or removing certain privileges. Ultimately, the intention is to teach the child that there are alternative, acceptable behaviours to achieve their needs without resorting to maladaptive ones.

6.4   SOCIAL/EMOTIONAL SELF-REGULATION

Sometimes, challenging behaviours arise from underlying social/emotional dysregulation. Typically, children learn to regulate their social and emotional responses over time. It is not uncommon for young children to feel distressed and to throw tantrums when they don't get their way. But it becomes maladaptive and dysregulated when the tantrums do not abide over time; or becomes intense and frequent that it affects the well-being of others around the child.

Challenging behaviours arising from social emotional dysregulation, can include anxiety, anger, obsessions etc. A child who gets highly anxious may not be able to tell others directly that he is anxious but could exhibit anxious behaviours such as not wanting to go to school, engaging in self injurious behaviours such as head banging, biting, crying easily, and even throwing tantrums that result in major meltdowns. It is also possible that expressions of physically and verbally aggressive behaviours, such as hitting others, biting others, shouting, throwing objects or swearing, mask underlying anxiety.

When we view such behaviours as responses that the child uses to cope with certain adverse environments or situations, then it makes sense for parents, teachers and caregivers to help the child learn more adaptive ways to respond, adapt and cope in those environments and situations. For an ASD child, anxiety and anger can stem from seemingly ordinary environments or situations. What may seem ordinary could be perceived as adverse, daunting or threatening by the child. Situations such as a last-minute change in schedule, adding something new to a schedule or even missing an old pair of socks could rile up the child and potentially trigger a meltdown. Researchers who have studied anxiety-related concerns among ASD children indicate that there is current evidence that point to the association between anxiety disorders and autism-related social deficits.

6.5 BEST PRACTICE INTERVENTIONS AND STRATEGIES

An intervention refers to a plan with clearly drawn-up goals and objectives that could be based on a specific treatment program or a treatment plan that is tailored specifically for the child by the therapist. On the other hand, strategies refer to the specific tools or techniques that are used to communicate with and teach the child.

A behavioural approach to intervention is often used in managing behaviours in ASD children who are intellectually disabled and lacking in language skills. Different treatment programs are now available that are essentially based on Applied Behaviour Analysis (ABA). These programs are often highly structured and intensive (of 30 to 40 hours a week), involves one-to-one direct instruction and are based purely on the principles of behaviour analysis and modification described earlier in the chapter.

For ASD children with strong verbal reasoning abilities, a cognitive-based approach such as Cognitive-Behaviour Therapy (CBT) is gaining strength of evidence among researchers. CBT involves teaching the child to use both their cognition and actions to alter their negative thought processes, emotions and actions. They are taught in a step-by-step manner to understand consequences of negative thoughts and to use alternative positive self-talk to monitor and alter their actions. CBT has been shown to be effective in helping verbal ASD children cope better with their emotional issues.

In practice, psychologists often use a modified form of CBT that takes into account the visual learning strengths of the ASD child. Use of pictures, diagrams, charts, visual cue cards and self-monitoring checklists are often integrated into a CBT program. Programmes widely used or adapted by psychologists in the field include CBT-based programs such the Cognitive Affective Training (CAT) kit developed by Tony Attwood, and the Cool Kids Programme developed at Macquarie University, Australia.

6.6   VISUALLY-BASED STRATEGIES WORK BEST

In order to carry out a behaviour intervention effectively, the use of specific strategies that tap into the learning strengths of ASD children is recommended. Most ASD children are better in their ability to process information visually. As such, visually-based supports and strategies are often used to help them learn concepts and social behaviour.

Visual supports and strategies can range from the very concrete to more abstract forms like comic strip drawing or social stories. Types of visual support and strategies include:

- real-life objects,
- pictures, charts, or diagrams,
- video clips,
- comic strip conversations,
- photographs,
- social stories.

Some parents think that visual supports are only relevant for ASD children who have limited verbal ability or that such supports should be dispensed with when they get older. The rationale underlying the use of such supports is to scaffold or help the ASD person understand or process what needs to be learned or communicated more efficiently.

For instance, teaching a child perspective taking or understanding how others think or feel is in itself an abstract task. Drawing it out in picture form (comic strip drawing) helps to transform abstract thoughts into some form of concrete representation. Social stories and comic strip conversations were first developed by Carol Gray (a teacher) as a teaching tool to help ASD children learn social cues, social skills, and manage their emotions. For more information about how they can be used, go to www.carolgraysocialstories.com

MEDICATION AND ASD

There is as yet no medication that can cure ASD. Generally speaking, medication has a limited role in improving social and communication difficulties. Currently, medication can be prescribed for some behavioural difficulties that result from other mental health conditions that the ASD child might have (mental health co-morbidities), such as Attention Deficit Hyperactivity Disorder (ADHD), anxiety, depression or aggressive behaviours. The use of medication may help to manage these difficulties such that the child may be able to better participate and benefit from community, educational and other services.

However, medication should only be prescribed by a specialised medical professional, such as a psychiatrist. Medication should be only considered after and in conjunction with behavioural and psychological management strategies. The use of medication should also be reviewed regularly.

7.1   AVAILABLE MEDICATIONS

Antipsychotics

Antipsychotics, as the name implies, are typically used in the management of psychotic conditions such as schizophrenia. However, at lower doses, they can also be used to reduce behaviours such as aggression, irritability and tics. There are two main groups of antipsychotics:

- Conventional antipsychotics
  - These medications are more likely to cause extrapyramidal side effects, such as tremors and stiffness.
  - Examples include Haloperidol, Chlorpromazine and Trifluoperazine (Stelazine).
- Atypical antipsychotics
  - These medications are more likely to cause metabolic side effects, such as weight gain, increased levels of blood glucose and lipids and high blood pressure.
  - Examples include Risperidone and Aripiprazole.

Antidepressants

These are used to manage depression, anxiety and obsessive-compulsive behaviours. There are two main categories of commonly used antidepressants:

- Selective Serotonin Reuptake Inhibitors (SSRIs)
  - Side effects include nausea, poor appetite, urinary retention, poor sleep and sexual dysfunction.
  - Examples include Fluoxetine (Prozac), Fluvoxamine (Faverin), Lexapro (Escitaolpram) and Sertraline (Zoloft).
- Tricyclic Antidepressants (TCAs)
  - Side effects include irregular heart rhythms (potentially fatal), dry mouth, blurred vision, constipation, urinary retention and drowsiness
  - Examples include Amitriptyline, Clomipramine and Imipramine.

Mood Stabilisers

These are usually used to stabilise mood variations in bipolar disorders and for epilepsy. In ASD, these medications can be also used to manage impulsivity, irritability and aggression. Examples include Sodium Valproate (Epilium) and Carbamazepine (Tegretol).

Stimulants/ Medications for Inattention and Hyperactivity

These are usually used for children with symptoms of ADHD. They improve alertness, attention and impulse control, and reduce excessive motor activity. In Singapore, the most commonly used stimulant is methylphenidate (Ritalin, Concerta). Stimulants typically have a rapid onset of action (about 30 minutes) and last for a specified number of hours within the day of administration. Common adverse effects include stomach discomfort, poor appetite, palpitations, changes in blood pressure, headache and insomnia.

Atomoxetine (Strattera) is a norepinephrine reuptake inhibitor used for those with ADHD. Unlike methylphenidate, atomoxetine requires about two to four weeks for effects to become apparent. Side effects include nausea, dry mouth, poor appetite, lethargy, palpitations, increase in blood pressure and mood changes.

Medications for Sleep

Many children with ASD have difficulty with sleep. Melatonin is a neuro-hormone that occurs naturally in our bodies that causes drowsiness. Melatonin supplements have been increasingly used to treat sleep disorders in children with ASD in recent years.

7.2   ADVERSE EFFECTS OF MEDICATION

All medications have potential side effects. It is important to weigh the potential benefits of medication against its side effects to help you decide if medication will be helpful for your child. Not every child on a particular medication will experience its potential side effects. Each medication has its own profile of side effects and your doctor will be able to advise you on which medication is suitable for your child.

7.3   RECENT RESEARCH IN MEDICATION FOR ASD

There are currently no medications that can treat the core social and communication deficits in autism. However, researchers are now looking into the possibility of using medication to manage these deficits. Examples of such agents include oxytocin, medications targeting glutamate receptors (such as Memantine) and Omega-3 fatty acids. However, these are all currently still in the early stages of research and are not used clinically as yet.

INTERVENTIONS ADDRESSING SPECIFIC NEEDS

PART 8

8.1   THE ROLE OF OCCUPATIONAL THERAPY

The doctor or psychologist may recommend occupational therapy for your child when he has been evaluated to have certain gross motor, fine motor and/or sensory processing difficulties. Early motor delays, difficulties with gross and fine motor coordination, and postural control may co-occur in children with ASD.

Occupational therapy uses activity-based interventions to help children cope with physical or environmental challenges of daily living. The occupational therapist (OT) will first assess your child's physiological milestones based on what he is expected to be able to achieve at his developmental age. Thereafter, the therapist discusses with primary caregivers and/or parents on an appropriate course of treatment. Treatment will often necessitate commitment on the part of the child and caregivers to undertake "homework" to address specific areas of difficulties, outside of therapy sessions.

Here are some examples of various types of difficulties that occupational therapy can help to address:

For a Child with Fine Motor Difficulties

The OT will evaluate specific areas such as overall pencil grip and control, the spatial organisation of space and letter formation, speed and dexterity etc. Treatment will focus on improving finger strength, hand strength, hand position and stability.

For the Child who is Hypotonic (Low Muscle Tone)

Treatment will focus more on developing gross motor skills through play, purposeful activities, heavy work and spatial movement.

For the Child with a Bilateral Co-ordination Problem

Treatment will focus more on improving coordination between both hands, both legs, and between the left and right sides of the body.

For the Child with a Praxis Problem

Praxis is the ability to plan and execute skilled movements. The individual with a praxis problem has difficulty planning his movements. Treatment will focus on improving motor skills, timing (which requires planning) and accuracy. Treatment under the care of an occupational therapist usually progresses slowly in order to let the child master one motor skill at a time. When a motor skill is finally acquired, the child usually can become very proficient in it.

Sensory Integration Therapy

Sensory integration is a process that allows us to take in information through the senses and put it into a form that helps us make sense of the environment.

In many children with ASD, the process of putting together these different stimuli from the environment seems to be somewhat impaired. They may be over- or under-reacting to environmental stimuli and hence have difficulty making sense of the information they get from the environment.

Here are some of the commonly seen behaviours that children with ASD and sensory integration difficulties exhibit:

- Walking on the toes.
- Hand flapping and other repetitive movements.
- Acute awareness of background noises.
- Fascination with lights, fans and water.
- Interest in making objects spin.
- Little awareness of pain or temperature.
- Extremes of activity level (either hyperactive or under-active).
- Striking out at someone who accidentally brushes by them.
- Avoiding physical contact with certain textures such as sand or finger paints.
- A strong dislike of certain grooming activities like having a haircut.
- An unusual sensitivity to sounds and smells.

Sensory integration therapy include therapies such as brushing and rubbing the body, touch therapy, deep pressure and compression of joints. There is insufficient evidence to support the effectiveness of this form of therapy for children with ASD. But anecdotal reports from parents indicate that for some children, it has helped them modulate their sensory functions better in everyday life.

OTs may also be able to give recommendations on ways to adapt, accommodate or minimise sensory reactions to environmental stimuli. For instance, ear muffs may benefit those who are sensitive to environmental noise; if a child is sensitive to certain types of fabrics, then avoiding those types of fabrics may be the solution.

8.2   THE ROLE OF SPEECH AND LANGUAGE THERAPY

When a child with ASD presents with severe difficulties in speech and/or verbal communication abilities, interventions undertaken by a Speech and Language Therapist is warranted. A spectrum of communication deficits in ASD children can range from non-existent verbal speech, to having a smattering of phrase speech, and to having difficulties understanding abstract, non-literal language. Early intervention (i.e. in preschool years) in communication difficulties will often see better gains for the child.

A speech-and-language therapist will first do a comprehensive assessment of the child's speech and language milestones and explore the current presenting issues that are impacting on the child's communicative skills. Thereafter, an plan or programme is tailored to suit the needs of the child.

Augmentative Alternative Communication (AAC) Tools

For children with severe speech impairments, the therapist determines the best program that is suitable for the child. Commonly used Augmentative Alternative Communication (AAC) tools include Picture Exchange Communication Systems (PECS) and Sign Language Training (SLT).

The primary goal of PECS is to establish and enhance spontaneous communication through the use of picture-based cards. It is a sequentially structured program built into six phases. The use of SLT may also be considered for children who have difficulty understanding two-dimensional visual representations of words.

Some parents may feel that using picture cards for daily communication needs is cumbersome and express concerns that their child will not be able to progress in verbal speech. It may seem counter-intuitive to use picture cards to communicate but there is growing research evidence that PECS can actually assist expressive language development and social communication skills, especially when they are used from an early age. AAC tools can help to expand language communication, as well as stimulate speech acquisition in non-verbal children.

Today, ACC apps are available on mobile and tablet devices, thus reducing the inconvenience of carrying thick folders of PECS cards.

Language-based Therapy to Improve Communicative Language Skills

Some ASD children who are verbal (able to speak in sentences) may present with difficulties comprehending and processing complex language in academic and social settings. Language-based interventions conducted by speech-and-language therapists may be able to ameliorate some of the difficulties by teaching abstract linguistic concepts more explicitly.

There is no single programme or method that works. Improvement in language skills also depends on factors such as continued practice and its use in home and school environments, the motivation of the child, and the child's developmental age.

8.3   COMPLEMENTARY ALTERNATIVE THERAPIES

There is a plethora of complementary and alternative therapies (CAT) that are practiced commercially outside of healthcare settings. In Singapore, the Ministry of Health (MOH) advises that "parents and caregivers should not replace mainstream interventions for preschool children with ASD with complementary and alternative therapies" (*AMS-MOH Clinical Practice Guidelines 2010*, 12 p. 65).

The Academy of Medicine and MOH have jointly reviewed some of these therapies and listed the following CATs that they do not recommended for preschool children with ASD because of insufficient, conflicting or inconclusive empirical evidence:

- Amino acid supplementation.
- Animal-assisted therapy.
- Behavioural optometry.
- Expressive psychotherapy.
- Gluten-free and/or casein-free diet.
- Sound therapies (Samonas Sound Therapy and the Listening Programme).
- Massage and other sensory-based intervention.
- Music therapy.
- Acupuncture.
- Cranio-sacral therapy.

The list is not exhaustive.

Caregivers are advised to exercise caution and weigh the risks and benefits. Some of these therapies are, in fact, undergoing more investigation and the findings may not have caught up with positive anecdotal reports. Notwithstanding, here are some factors can be considered when deciding on CATs:

- Does the CAT add value to an existing mainstream intervention?
- Will spending the time, money and effort produce the desired results in the long run?
- Are there any potential harmful effects?
- Does it improve the child's quality of life?

EDUCATIONAL APPROACHES IN SINGAPORE

PART 9

In Singapore, teachers and professionals working with children/individuals with ASD tend to adopt diverse approaches in planning their educational programmes. Some of the key approaches are Applied Behavioural Analysis (ABA), TEACCH Structured Teaching and Developmental Models.

9.1   APPLIED BEHAVIOURAL ANALYSIS (ABA)

ABA is a scientific method that enhances appropriate and useful behaviours, and reduces problematic ones. Every skill is broken down into small, discrete steps and taught in a precise and systematic way. It is an individualised and intensive behavioural approach, with a therapist working individually with one child up to many hours a week. ABA, if it is offered privately, is an expensive treatment programme that will place significant financial strains on families.

An ABA-based treatment programme focuses on a variety of skills a person requires so as to function independently. These include language, social skills, play skills, academic skills and self-help skills. Children are actively and explicitly taught, for example, how to pay attention, imitate, use communicative language (be it verbal or through picture communication), show and receive affection, and relate to other children.

This behavioural approach is particularly useful for children who present with maladaptive or challenging behaviours. A functional behavioural analysis of the target behaviour is implemented, in which the child's reinforcements are identified and behavioural strategies are implemented to promote desired alternative behaviours. Results from current research have demonstrated efficacy in addressing problem behaviours and in facilitating communication, social skills, functional living skills and learning.

9.2   TEACCH STRUCTURED TEACHING

This is an approach developed by the Treatment and Education of Autistic and related Communication-handicapped Children (TEACCH). This programme was developed in the US in the early 1970s by Eric Schopler from the University of North Carolina. It focuses on the individual with ASD, his or her skills, interests and needs, and it strives to provide supportive task environments. Structures, which are usually presented visually, indicate: "What task?", "When to start?", "When to finish?", "Where?", "How to do?", "With whom?" and "What's next?"

The aim of TEACCH is to build on the child's strengths and interests rather than concentrating and drilling on his deficits. This helps to increase the child's motivation and understanding of what is being done. TEACCH also encompasses other aspects of life, including social and leisure activities. It also aims to carry the same principles over the individual's lifetime so that he is able to function in a chosen vocation independently. Hence, the ultimate aim of TEACCH is to help the individual function meaningfully and independently.

Existing literature that came from case studies and research on parent teaching and feedback from professionals reported strengths in this approach. Currently, the principles of TEACCH Structured Teaching are commonly adopted in special education schools, in some mainstream schools, day activity centres and at home.

9.3 DEVELOPMENTAL MODELS

Two developmental models available in Singapore, often provided by private centres, are Developmental Individual-difference, Relationship-based (DIR) or Floortime and Relationship Development Intervention (RDI). These models aim to promote socio-emotional growth and relationship building. Research on the effectiveness of these models have remained inconclusive thus far.

LEARNING NEEDS OF
CHILDREN WITH ASD

PART 10

'Many people with special needs can be trained and become contributing members of the workforce, if they receive timely and effective early intervention and education'
– Ms Denise Phua (Today, 7 February 2015)

Every child has a right to be educated. Whether a child has ASD or not, has a superior IQ or learning difficulties, all of them have a potential to learn and develop. Whether the child with ASD is high-functioning or with intellectual disabilities, the child has his own unique set of interests, strengths and challenges.

Children with ASD are likely to benefit from structured educational approach with individualised education plan to enhance their verbal and non-verbal skills, academic, social skills, motor skills and behavioural adaptations. Early intervention programmes are likely to enhance a child's readiness to learning and formal schooling.

In Singapore, various school settings are available to support children based on their intellectual abilities and extent of their special needs once they reach the age for formal schooling. Mainstream schools provide support in terms of specially trained personnel who are only equipped to support ASD children with mild learning needs. On the other hand, there are special education schools that are suitably equipped to support ASD children with intellectual disabilities and special learning needs.

Parents/caregivers may wish to find out more about early intervention programmes, mainstream schools, special schools and/or day activity centres from the following websites:

- Early Intervention Programmes
  - www.sgenable.sg
- Mainstream Schools
  - www.moe.gov.sg/education/programmes/support-for-children-special-needs/
- Special Education Schools
  - www.moe.gov.sg/education/special-education/schoollist/
- Day Activity Centres
  - www.sgenable.sg

10.1 EARLY INTERVENTION PROGRAMMES

The Early Intervention Programme for Infants & Children (EIPIC) centres in Singapore aim to provide early intervention for children diagnosed with disabilities aged 6 years old and below. Some of the centres that cater to young children with ASD are the Eden Children's Centre, Rainbow Centre, WeCan Early Intervention Programme, Early Years Centre (AWWA), THK EIPIC Centre, Fei Yu EIPIC Centre and Metta Pre-School. In general, the EIPIC programmes aim to equip the young children with the motor, communication, self-help, social development, basic literacy and numeracy skills. The programmes may range from two to three times per week, and from two to three hours per session. Government funding is available to help defray the early intervention fees. Parents can also tap on the Baby Bonus scheme to offset the EIPIC fees. There are also some privately run centres that provide early intervention programmes.

10.2 MAINSTREAM SCHOOLS

In 2005, the Ministry of Education (MOE) started an initiative to support children with mild Special Educational Needs (SEN) in mainstream schools. Currently, all primary schools have been staffed with at least one Allied Educator (Learning and Behavioural Support), or AED (LBS), to support students with mild special needs. Currently, there are 69 secondary schools are resourced to support students with mild special needs. AEDs (LBS) support students with mild special educational needs such as dyslexia, Autism Spectrum Disorder (ASD) and Attention Deficit Hyperactivity Disorder (ADHD). In addition, all schools have a core group of Teachers trained in Special Needs (TSNs) to support students with mild SEN. As of end of 2013, 10% of teachers in all primary school and 20% of teachers in all secondary school have been trained in special needs.

The specific roles of the AEDs (LBS) and TSNs are outlined in the MOE website. For instance, the AED (LBS) can provide individual/small group intervention support (e.g. in literacy skills) as well as small group skills training (e.g. social skills, study and organisational skills etc). They work with class teachers, and School Counsellors to support students' learning needs. The role of the TSN includes sharing strategies and resources with other teachers and parents, and assisting with the transition of students with mild SEN from one grade level to the next.

Facilitating Adjustment to School

Whilst some structural support is in place in schools, children with ASD may require additional support from parents and teachers to cope adequately in school. Parents may need to be proactive in advocating for their child while being diplomatic and working with teachers as partners. Working with the child's teachers can be helpful in developing supports for him in school and alleviating some of the difficulties he may be experiencing.

Parents should keep the school informed of any specialised help or intervention programmes that their child has outside of school. It would be helpful to work closely with the class teacher and the AED to monitor their child's performance, not just in his grades but in terms of how effective he in assimilating class lessons, completing assignments, organising himself and interacting with classmates.

Some possible classroom behavioural support tools include:
- seating the child near the front row of the class,
- the use of visual representation to explain sequence of the class activities (e.g. using picture symbols pasted on strip or written schedule to help child understand the sequence of activities),
- the use of visual behavioural cues to prompt expected behaviours (e.g. having picture cues of "quiet", "sit down" or "listen"),
- the use of environmental support or physical structure (e.g. paste coloured tape on the floor to indicate circle time area, reading corner or chill-out corner),
- setting up a request for assistance system, whereby the child can indicate to school personnel when he or she needs help, feels distressed or wishes to see the AED, counsellor or psychologist (e.g. the child can flash a card to indicate "I need help" or "I wish to go the counsellor room"),
- setting up a chill-out corner for the child to use when distressed,
- working out "differentiated homework" for the child that he can better cope with,
- setting up buddy system, whereby a few students befriend a child, remind him or her on what need to be done and offer assistance when necessary,
- facilitating the child to read social cues and manage teasing,

- encouraging the child to share with you the names of the classmates whom he plays or interacts with,
- teaching the child play skills (e.g. how to play catch, pretend play or simple board games),
- teaching the child how to respond to teasing (e.g. use sentence scripts like "don't disturb me", "leave me alone" or "stop it"),
- if teasing is still persistent: inform the child's form teacher, find out what is happening in school and allow school personnel to manage the situation.

Special Examination Accommodations

Some children in mainstream schools may require accommodations for tests and examinations, especially for national examinations such as the Primary School Leaving Examination (PSLE) and the GCE 'N' or 'O' Level examinations in Singapore.

Parents should discuss with teachers if their child needs special accommodations such as extended time in exams, having a prompter, rest breaks or separate seating.

Home Support

Children with ASD face many challenges in the mainstream school setting. Apart from having to keep up with academics that the typical student has to cope with, the ASD child also has to organise and plan for himself, adjust to changes in the environment and cope with social-communication demands.

Home support is hence pivotal in helping the ASD child cope with schooling. Parents should firstly understand their child's interests, strengths and difficulties and adjust their expectations according to their child's abilities. They should create a supportive home environment that will maximise his or her strengths. They should give him or her time to acquire knowledge and skills that may not come so easily for him or her and where possible create opportunities to apply the knowledge or skills acquired.

Possible areas to work on:
- Create a positive learning environment, use rewards or positive reinforcements to motivate child in his or her learning.
- Create opportunities for child to learn and improve on his adaptive

functioning skills such as toilet training, putting on clothes, taking a shower, eating meals independently or making simple meals.
- Create opportunities for the child to learn and acquire literacy and numeracy in practical ways. For example, prompt the child to read food menus and order food.
- Start off with simple tasks that can be completed with success.
- Break up tasks or learning into small segments to reduce stress and promote compliance.
- Support verbal instructions with visual representations and/or hands-on learning.

Online resources for teaching:
- Autism Speaks on teaching important life skills
  - www.autismspeaks.org/family-services/community-connections/teaching-important-life-skills
- Do2Learn: Educational Resources for Special Needs
  - www.do2learn.com/

10.3 AUTISM-FOCUSED SCHOOL OFFERING MAINSTREAM EDUCATION

Pathlight School was established by the Autism Resource Centre (Singapore) at the invitation of the Ministry of Education (MOE) in 2004. It is the first autism-focused school in Singapore that offers the local mainstream academic curriculum together with life skills. It caters to students with mild to moderate autism, aged 7 to 18 years old, who are cognitively able to access mainstream academic curriculum but who may require additional support such as smaller class sizes, special accommodations and teaching staff trained in autism. For more information about the school, please refer to www.pathlight.org.sg

10.4 SPECIAL EDUCATION SCHOOLS (SPED)

There are currently 20 SPED schools run by 13 Voluntary Welfare Organisations (VWOs) with funding from the Ministry of Education (MOE) and the National Council of Social Service (NCSS). These SPED schools customise their programmes to cater to students with intellectual disabilities and related developmental and physical disabilities. A child with an IQ that is well below average is classified as having intellectual disability. Intellectual disability refers to below-average intellectual functioning and demonstrated by IQ scores below a standard score of 70. Children of very low IQ have significant difficulties adapting to their roles as students in a school that has a curriculum that caters to students who are in the average and above-average intellectual functioning.

All things considered, helping children with intellectual disabilities is about recognising that vocational training and adaptive life skills take precedence over academic achievements. These children need training in life skills in order to cope with day-to-day living. Education for them should be aimed at attaining functional skills. Usually when they reach adolescence, the training should aim towards helping them find a suitable job or vocation that will enable them to lead independent adult lives.

10.5 DAY ACTIVITY CENTRES

The Day Activity Centres (DACs) aim to support individuals with disabilities, within the age range of 16 to 55 years old and who are not ready for employment and/ or independent living. In general, the centres provide training and coaching to equip individuals with disabilities with the life skills to promote independent living.

Some of the programmes include literacy and money skills, social development, communication, and physical and leisure skills. For those who demonstrate work readiness and have the necessary life skills, the centres may prepare them for sheltered employment. Some of the centres that cater to individuals with ASD in Singapore are the Eden Centre for Adults, St Andrew's Autism Centre, Bizlink Day Activity Centre and MINDS Training Development Centres. Family members can choose to sign up their adult with ASD for a full-day or half-day programme, from Monday to Friday. Like the EIPIC centres, government funding is available to help offset the centres' fees.

10.6 DECIDING ON A SCHOOL FOR YOUR CHILD

Look at the long-term big picture. Consider variables in your child's overall profile such has his language abilities, cognitive abilities, daily functioning needs, motivation and ability to learn when deciding on the most appropriate educational setting. Some parents tend to set the bar high in terms of academic expectations for their child. Invariably, there is a culturally-ingrained mindset in Singapore that seems to measure success in term of academic performance. However, we can't always use academic performance as the single yardstick in measuring the child's success and well-being, and in the process, overlook other aspects of his life. Sometimes, much emotional distress and frustration are generated within the family just because the child fails to meet the academic expectations foisted by parents and teachers.

Parents would need to ensure that the child has a positive learning experience in school and grows in his functional learning and daily living skills. The focus should be on raising a happy child who learns to accept himself with his pattern of strengths and difficulties. Some of the factors to consider in the selection of an appropriate school for a child with ASD would be the child's cognitive abilities, behavioural profile and the level of support that he may require to cope adequately.

COPING WITH ASD IN THE FAMILY

PART 11

Having a child with ASD is likely to have significant impact on any family. Some of the stressors include emotional stress, financial stress, coping with the behavioural challenges, adjustment in family life, restriction of social lives and worry about the child's future. During the early phase of diagnosis, parents are likely to experience grief, anger and despair. Such feelings are understandable and to be expected. These feelings may re-emerge at different phases of the child's life such as child's transition to formal schooling, transition to vocational training or during major family events.

11.1 PARENTS' COPING AND HOPES

Seeking information on ASD and appropriate intervention services for child are some of the initial adaptations in coping with the diagnosis of ASD. Existing literature has shown that early intervention is likely to make a difference in how children learn new skills and adapt to the social environment. Hope and positive outlook help to keep parents and families going.

Studies have shown that what helps to sustain parents' hope and resilience in caring for their child are understanding and support between spouses, family support, coaching from helping professionals, support from other parents with special-needs children, religious faith, acceptance of their child's disability and acknowledgement of their child's strengths and achievements. Parents and families need time, appropriate information and courage to keep moving forward.

In addition to seeking information from the helping professionals, parents can have access to information on ASD from the following websites and training providers:

- Autism Spectrum Disorder in Pre-School Children
  - AMS-MOH Clinical Practice Guidelines
  - www.moh.gov.sg
- Autism Resource Centre
  - On Autism Resources and Training Calendar
    www.autism.org.sg
- Autism Association (Singapore)
  - www.autismlinks.org.sg
- Rainbow Centre
  - Training and Consultancy
    www.rainbowcentre.org.sg

- SSI Social Service Institute
  – Training Programmes
  www.socialserviceinstitute.sg

11.2 SEEKING PROFESSIONAL SUPPORT AND COUNSELLING

Every child with ASD is unique and special. Some may be compliant and attentive. Some may present with challenging behaviours such as hyperactivity, anxiety, frequent outbursts or meltdowns. It is important to seek appropriate treatment and/or medical consultation for the management of ASD and co-morbid conditions.

Caring for a child with ASD can be a formidable task for some families and sometimes it may at take a toll on the caregivers' emotional well-being. If caregivers should experience depressive moods or irritability for a period of time, it is important to seek counselling and/or specialist advice.

Below are some community resources on mental health:

- Health Promotion Board
  – Mental Health & Where to Seek Help
  www.hpb.gov.sg
- Family Services Centres
  – Counselling service
  app.msf.gov.sg/dfcs/familyservice/default.aspx

11.3 UNDERSTANDING SIBLINGS' PERSPECTIVES

Siblings of children with ASD may learn from a young age that their brother or sister is different from other "typical" children based on their parents' responses and their own interaction with their brother or sister. They may wonder why their brother or sister is unable to play or relate with them or they may feel embarrassed by his or her behaviours in public. It is not uncommon for the siblings to experience moments of sadness, resentfulness, confusion, loneliness or jealousy towards their brother or sister. With gentle guidance and appropriate explanation, most siblings do learn to overcome their mixed feelings over time. It is important to acknowledge the siblings' feelings, make time for them and support them accordingly.

Some possible areas to address with siblings of a child with ASD:

- Explain what ASD is. Information shared should be appropriate to the siblings' developmental level.

- Address the siblings' frustrations or jealousy when they perceive parents spending not enough time with them as compared to the child with ASD or parents being "unfair" in the management of misbehaviours.
- Acknowledge the siblings' concerns when their personal belongings such as books, toys or games are damaged by the child with ASD.
- Teach siblings what they can say or how they can explain to their friends about the child with ASD so that they do not feel embarrassed or lost when asked.
- Play and spend time with the siblings. It is important to spend time alone with the siblings as well as time together as a family.
- Support and maximise the siblings' potential.

11.4 ROLE OF GRANDPARENTS

In general, parents should take on the primary role in caring for their children. However, grandparents can supplement parents' efforts and provide assistance in the areas of childcare, household chores and offer advice and encouragement. Where possible, grandparents should have access to information on ASD and learn strategies and techniques on how to educate or manage the behaviours of the child with ASD. These will provide consistency in the management of the child's behaviours. Grandparents' acceptance of the child with ASD will help to normalise the family's experience of having a child with special needs, thus contributing to the family's outlook for the future.

Below are some useful resources for families:
- The National Autistic Society
  - Living with Autism
    www.autism.org.uk/living-with-autism.aspx
- Autism Speaks
  - www.autismspeaks.org/

MY CHILD'S FUTURE

PART 12

Over the last decade, the development of ASD services in Singapore has progressed significantly. More government initiatives and funding have been introduced to support children with ASD in the early intervention programmes, special schools and mainstream schools. Studies show that effective education makes a substantial difference in the development of those with ASD. More children with ASD and average cognitive abilities progress to post-secondary education and open employment. Those with mild intellectual disability may have access to vocational training and/or supported employment. However, those with ASD and severe intellectual disability may require long-term assistance and support.

12.1 MAXIMISING MY CHILD'S POTENTIAL

A good understanding of ASD and your child's impairments in the areas of social interaction, communication and stereotyped patterns of behaviours is essential in supporting your child. With appropriate intervention and over time, some do show improvements in their social interaction, communication and behaviours. However, for some, their impairments may present differently over the course of time. For example, some children may not be keen to interact with unfamiliar people when younger but do respond to social approaches as they grow older.

Existing literature have shown that a significant proportion of children with ASD have intellectual disability. For some children, language acquisition is a long process and among them some may not fully attain flexible speech even in their adulthood. For this group of children, they may benefit from using augmentative communication tools such as Picture Exchange Communication (PEC) and these tools should be made available to them even up to their adulthood.

For children with ASD, it is important to focus not just on academic learning but also on functional life skills. When they are young, it is essential to focus on self-care skills, functional communication, leisure skills and play skills. As they progress to adolescence and adulthood, it is necessary to address some of the developmental, emotional and physiological changes such as their sense of identity, sexuality and feelings, friendships and sexual relationship, academic demands and vocational inclination.

12.2 ADOLESCENCE AND ADULTHOOD

Studies have shown that the outlook for a child with ASD is influenced by his access to appropriate educational intervention, his cognitive ability and his behavioural profile. Placement in a mainstream school may not necessary be beneficial for children with ASD. It is important to understand and accept your child's potential, decide on an education setting that will best fit your child and groom him in areas that he demonstrates some strength and interest.

For Individuals with ASD and Intellectual Disability

Appropriate educational placement will certainly help to reduce the child's frustrations and contribute to his acquisitions of knowledge and skills at a pace that is suitable for him. Due to the physiological and emotional changes during the adolescence phase, some individuals with ASD, impaired cognitive abilities and/or lacking the verbal skills may present behavioural challenges. This is a phase when the adolescent or adult may want some autonomy and become less receptive to adults' instructions as compared to when they are younger. They may show their displeasure in temper tantrums, meltdowns or physical aggression. Physically the adolescent or adult with ASD may be stronger and taller than their parents or teachers. Direct confrontation is not advisable.

The adolescent or adult should be meaningfully engaged in educational, vocational and leisure activities that are developmentally age-appropriate and that take into account their interests and aptitudes. His daily activities should be structured, predictable and presented visually so as to facilitate understanding and compliance. Where appropriate, the individual should be given options or opportunities to exercise his choice. For example, the individual should be given some options to decide on his preferred leisure activities, clothing or food. Sexual development and puberty can be a challenging period for some individuals with ASD and their families. Issues of physical changes to the body, hygiene and body fluids, appropriate or inappropriate touch, masturbation or use of sanitary pads need to be explicitly taught. Some parents report that their adolescents behave differently at home and in school. Usually, they may be calmer or more compliant in school than at home, or vice versa. Therefore, communication and collaboration between parents and school personnel will certainly help to optimise the individual's and family's functioning.

For Individuals with ASD and Adequate Cognitive Ability

More and more individuals with ASD and adequate cognitive ability do progress from primary, secondary to tertiary education. The academic demands in Singapore mainstream schools are widely considered stressful for most students. For those with ASD, their stress level may be elevated not only with coping with the examinations stress but also by the social and communicative demands of school. Some adolescents may face challenges in getting along with their peers, doing group projects and/or making oral presentations. Some may have difficulty juggling with the many subjects in the secondary or tertiary level. Others may require academic and counselling support to cope with school demands.

High-functioning adults with ASD may have a wide range of occupations. However, some may be less flexible with changes or less savvy in their social interaction and thus will require understanding and accommodation by their employers and colleagues. Some adults may desire to enter into relationships, but lack the know-how, and will require information and coaching on the social norms and rules.

Born with it, different from the rest
Struggled all the way, we tried our best
At times we're driven to the wall
Some of us fly some did fall.

As fellow humans we need help
Instead, society squashed us like kelp
Feared, mocked and sneered at
Labels, nicknames, aplenty we've had.

Had enough of discrimination
People out there, take caution
With willpower in the mind
With energy undefined.
Behold, just wait and see
This carp into a dragon would be!

by **Yiu On TANG**
who has mild traits of autism
(16 July 2003)

WHERE CAN I GO FOR HELP?

PART 13

DIAGNOSTIC ASSESSMENT AND INTERVENTION

FOR PRESCHOOLERS
Department of Child Development
KK Women's and Children's Hospital
100 Bukit Timah Road, Level 5 Women's Tower, Singapore 229899
Appointment Tel.: 6294 4050
www.kkh.com.sg

Child Development Unit@Jurong Medical Centre
NUH Kids, National University Hospital
Jurong Medical Centre
60 Jurong West Central 3, Singapore 648346.
Appointment Tel.: 6665 2530/6665 2531
www.nuh.com.sg

FOR SCHOOL-GOING CHILDREN / ADOLESCENTS
Child Guidance Clinic, IMH
Department of Child and Adolescent Psychiatry
Institute of Mental Health
Buangkok Green Medical Park
10 Buangkok View, Block 3, Basement 1, Singapore 539747.
IMH Appointment Tel.: 6389 2200
IMH Enquiry Tel.: 6389 2000
www.imh.com.sg

Child Guidance Clinic, HPB
Department of Child and Adolescent Psychiatry
Health Promotion Board Building, 3 Second Hospital Avenue, #03-01
Singapore 168937

Psychological Services Branch
Ministry of Education
51 Grange Road Blk 1 Level 3, Singapore 249564
Enquiry Tel.: 6388 6635
(Referral for diagnosis is made through school)

FOR ADULTS
Intellectual Disability Clinic
Adults Neuro-developmental Services
Institute of Mental Health
Buangkok Green Medical Park, 10 Buangkok View, Singapore 539747
IMH Appointment Tel.: 6389 2200
IMH Enquiry Tel.: 6389 2000

ORGANISATIONS
Autism Resource Centre (Singapore)
5 Ang Mo Kio Avenue 10, Singapore 569739
Enquiry Tel.: 6323 3258
www.autism.org.sg

Autism Association (Singapore)
101 Bukit Batok West Avenue 3, #01-01, Singapore 659168
Enquiry Tel.: 6774 6649
www.autismlinks.org.sg

Ministry of Education, Singapore
1 North Buona Vista Drive, Singapore 138675
Enquiry Tel.: 6872 2220
Special Education in Singapore
www.moe.gov.sg/education/special-education/
Support for Children with Special Education Needs
www.moe.gov.sg/education/programmes/

SG Enable
141 Redhill Road, Singapore 158828.
Enquiry Tel.: 1800 8585 885
www.sgenable.sg

SPEECH AND LANGUAGE THERAPY
Speech-Language and Hearing Association of Singapore
For information on speech and language therapy services
www.shas.org.sg

OCCUPATIONAL THERAPY
Singapore Association of Occupational Therapists
For information on occupational therapy services
www.saot.org.sg/

THERAPY SERVICES
THK Children's Therapy Centre
150A Mei Chin Road #02-01, Singapore 140150
Enquiry Tel.: 6471 4270
www.thkmc.org.sg/thk-childrens-therapy-centre/

SPD Therapy Hub
SPD Ability Centre
2 Peng Nguan Street, Singapore 168955.
Enquiry Tel.: 6570 0793/6579 0700
www.spd.org.sg/spd-therapy-hub.html

PSYCHOLOGICAL SERVICES
Singapore Psychological Society
For information on psychological services
www.singaporepsychologicalsociety.com

Students Care Service

Educational Psychology
Hougang Centre (Headquarter)
463 Hougang Ave 10, #01-964, Singapore 530463
Enquiry Tel.: 6286 9905
For information on the branches
www.students.org.sg

Care Corner

Educational Therapy Service
Blk 149 Toa Payoh Lor 1, #01-973, Singapore 310149
Enquiry Tel.: 6259 8683
For information on the education support and branches
www.carecorner.org.sg

NIE Wellness Centre

Psychological Studies
National Institute of Education
Psychological Studies Academic Group
1 Nanyang Walk, NIE2-B1-01/02, Singapore 637616
Appointment Tel.:6790 3318
www.ps.nie.edu.sg/WELLNESS.htm

Clinical and Health Psychology Centre

Department of Psychology
National University of Singapore
University Health Centre (Basement Level)
National University of Singapore
20 Lower Kent Ridge Road, Singapore 119080.
Enquiry Tel.: 6516 5322
www.fas.nus.edu.sg/psy/_clinical/chpc.htm

COUNSELING SERVICES

Singapore Association for Counseling

For information on counseling services
www.sac-counsel.org.sg

Family Service Centres

For a list of Family Service Centres
app.msf.gov.sg/dfcs/familyservice/default.aspx

Counseling and Care Centre

Blk 536 Upper Cross Street
#05-241 Hong Lim Complex, Singapore 050536
Enquiry Tel.: 6536 6366
www.counsel.org.sg

USEFUL RESOURCES

Gray C. (2010) *The New Social Story Book. Revised and Expanded 10th Anniversary Edition*. Arlington: Future Horizon.

Grandin T. & Panek R. (2013) *The Autistic Brain: Helping Different Kinds of Minds Succeed*. New York: Houghton Mifflin Harcourt Publishing Company

Jordan R. (2001) *Autism with Severe Learning Difficulties*. London: Souvenir Press (Educational & Academic) Ltd.

Notbohm E & Zysk V. (2010) *1001 Great Ideas for Teaching & Raising Children with Autism or Asperger's (Rev. and exp. 2nd ed.)* Arlington: Future Horizon.

Sung M. (2002) *My Brother is Different*. Singapore Institute of Mental Health.

Singapore Ministry of Health. (2010) *Autism Spectrum Disorders in Pre-School Children. AMS-MOH Clinical Practice Guidelines 1/2010*.

Tham-Toh JSY, Lyen K, Poon KK et al. (2012) *Rainbow Dreams: A Holistic Approach to Helping Children with Special Needs (3rd ed.)* Rainbow Centre, Singapore.

Tan B. (2010) *Come Into My World: 31 Stories of Autism in Singapore*. Singapore: Brenda Tan.

Volkmar F & Wiesner LA. (2009) *A Practical Guide to Autism: What Every Parent, Family Member and Teacher Needs to Know*. New Jersey: John Wiley & Sons, Inc.

Wing L. (2001) *The Autistic Spectrum: A Parent's Guide to Understanding and Helping Your Child*. Berkeley, CA: Ulysess Press.

REFERENCES

American Psychiatric Association. (2000). *Diagnostic and Statistical Manual of Mental Disorders (4th ed.)*. Washington, DC

American Psychiatric Association. (2013). *Diagnostic and Statistical Manual of Mental Disorders (5th ed.)*. Washington, DC

Academy of Medicine (AMS)-Ministry of Health (MOH) Clinical Practice Guidelines. (01/2010) *Autism Spectrum Disorders in Pre-school Children*. Ministry of Health, Singapore.

Volkmar F, et al. (2014) *Practice Parameter for the Assessment and Treatment of Children and Adolescents with Autism Spectrum Disorder*. Journal of the American Academy of Child and Adolescent Psychiatry, 53,2.

World Health Organisation. (1992) *International Statistical Classification of Diseases and Related Health Problems, 10th Revision (ICD-10)*. Geneva: WHO.

ABOUT THE AUTHORS

Dr. Sung Min

Dr Sung Min is a Senior Consultant at the Department of Child and Adolescent Psychiatry, Institute of Mental Health (Singapore), where she is the Programme Director of the Neuro-Behavioural Clinic (Autism Services and ADHD Services). She is also a Senior Clinical Lecturer at the Yong Loo Lin School of Medicine.

She obtained her Master of Medicine (Psychiatry) from the School of Postgraduate Medicine (National University of Singapore) and obtained her Advanced Specialist Training in Psychiatry in 2004. In 2005, Dr. Sung received the Healthcare Manpower Development Plan Fellowship Award and was attached to the Autism and Related Disorders Team at the Michael Rutter Centre for Children and Young People at the Institute of Psychiatry, United Kingdom.

Dr Sung is involved in local research projects on Autism Spectrum Disorder. She is an Independent Trainer in the Autism Diagnostic Interview — Revised and the Autism Diagnostic Observation Schedule.

Lena Heng

Ms Heng read Psychology for her undergraduate studies and obtained a B.Soc. Sci (Hons) from the National University of Singapore. Through her undergraduate studies, Ms Heng found her interest in autism and developmental disorders and did her honours research on teaching language to children with autism. Upon graduation, she worked as a psychologist at the Child Guidance Clinic, Institute of Mental Health. During her stint there, she co-authored the first edition of this book.

Equally interested in music, Lena has since went on to further her studies in music and is currently a full-time musician as well as a lecturer at the Nanyang Academy of Fine Arts.